BLAZERS

WEAPONS OF WAR

WEAPONS OF THE
COLD WAR

by Matt Doeden

Content Consultant:
Raymond L. Puffer, PhD
Retired Historian
United States Air Force

Reading Consultant:
Barbara J. Fox
Reading Specialist
North Carolina State University

Capstone
press

Mankato, Minnesota

Blazers is published by Capstone Press,
151 Good Counsel Drive, P.O. Box 669, Mankato, Minnesota 56002.
www.capstonepress.com

Library of Congress Cataloging-in-Publication Data
Doeden, Matt.
   Weapons of the Cold War / by Matt Doeden.
   p. cm. — (Blazers. Weapons of war)
   Includes bibliographical references and index.
   Summary: "Describes weapons of the Cold War, including nuclear weapons, missiles, and
defenses" — Provided by publisher.
   ISBN-13: 978-1-4296-2332-2 (hardcover)
   ISBN-10: 1-4296-2332-2 (hardcover)
   1. Nuclear warfare — Juvenile literature. 2. Cold war — Juvenile literature. I. Title.
U263.D63 2008
623.4'511909045 — dc22   2008030822

Editorial Credits

Mandy Robbins, editor; Alison Thiele, set designer; Kyle Grenz, book designer;
   Jo Miller, photo researcher

Photo Credits

AP Images, 10; Dan Grossi, 6–7; Dmitry Lovetsky, 12
Corbis/Bettmenn, 29 (Patriot missile launch)
Corel, 18–19, 23 (MiG-29)
DEFENSEIMAGERY.MIL, cover (aircraft), 22 (MiG-25), 22 (B-2); 23 (B-52); 29 (ASAT);
   PH2 Daniel McLain, USN, 22 (F-117); Staff Sgt Bill Thompson, 22 (B-1);
   Tech Sgt Michael Haggerty, 23 (SR-71)
Getty Images Inc./Ethan Miller, 21; Hulton Archive, 11; Central Press, 15; Time Life Pictures/
   Walter Sanders, 28
Nuclear Weapon Archive, 8–9
Shutterstock/Ivan Cholakov, 23 (MiG-17); photobank.kiev.ua/Mike Tolstoy, cover (rocket);
   Putchenko Kirill Victorovich, 13 (anti-aircraft missiles)
SuperStock, Inc., 4–5
The Image Works/ClassicStock/H. Armstrong Roberts, cover (fallout shelter), 29 (fallout shelter);
   Topham, 24, 29 (satellite); Photri, 27
U.S. Air Force photo, 16–17; by Master Sgt Rose Reynolds, 23 (U-2); by Staff Sgt Aaron D.
   Allmon II, 20
Wikipedia, public-domain image, 13 (nuclear bomb), 13 (nuclear warhead)

1 2 3 4 5 6 14 13 12 11 10 09

TABLE OF CONTENTS

THE WAR THAT WASN'T

During the cold war (1945–1989), the United States and the Soviet Union prepared for war. They built weapons and made battle plans. But no battles were ever fought.

missile factory

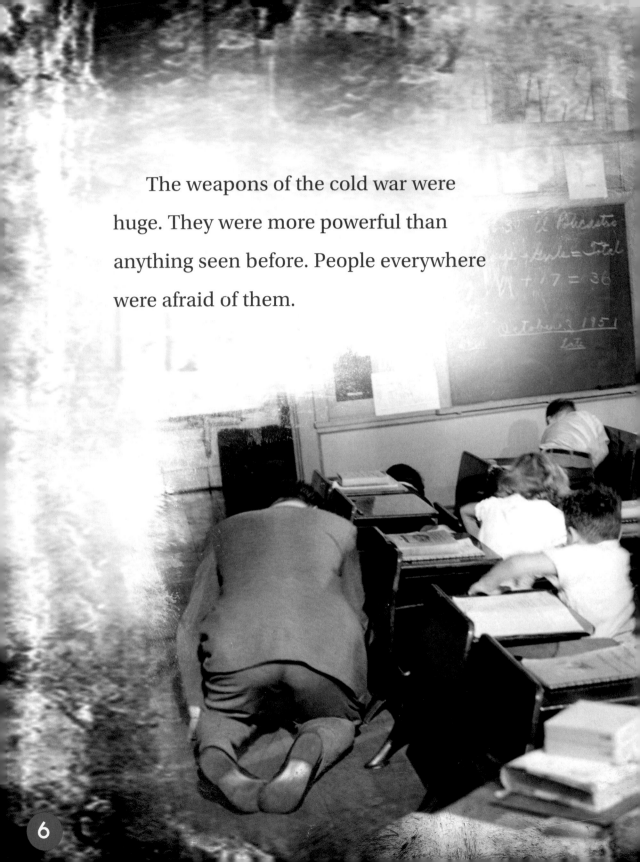

The weapons of the cold war were huge. They were more powerful than anything seen before. People everywhere were afraid of them.

WEAPON FACT

During the cold war, schoolchildren in the United States prepared for attacks. They practiced drills to duck and cover.

nuclear explosion

MIGHTY BOMBS AND MISSILES

Each country built hundreds of **nuclear bombs**. One bomb could destroy an entire city.

nuclear bomb — a powerful explosive that destroys large areas and leaves behind harmful particles called radiation

Missiles carried nuclear **warheads**. An Intercontinental Ballistic Missile (ICBM) could travel halfway around the world.

warhead — the explosive part of a missile

Russian ICBM

U.S. Atlas ICBM

WEAPON FACT

The most common U.S. ICBM was
the LGM-30 Minuteman III. It could
travel 6,000 miles (9,656 kilometers).

Submarines crept beneath the ocean surface. They carried Submarine Launched Ballistic Missiles (SLBMs).

WEAPON FACT

Submarines called boomers could shoot nuclear missiles.

Russian Typhoon submarine

EXPLOSIVES

nuclear bomb

nuclear warhead

anti-aircraft missiles

AWESOME AIRPLANES

Spy planes took photos of enemy actions from high in the sky. In the 1950s, the United States built the U-2 spy plane. The Soviet Union built the Yak-25.

U-2 spy plane

SR-71 Blackbird

The U.S. SR-71 Blackbird spy plane was hard for enemies to spot. It was the fastest plane ever built. Its top speed was faster than three times the speed of sound.

WEAPON FACT

The speed of sound at sea level is 761 miles (1,225 kilometers) per hour.

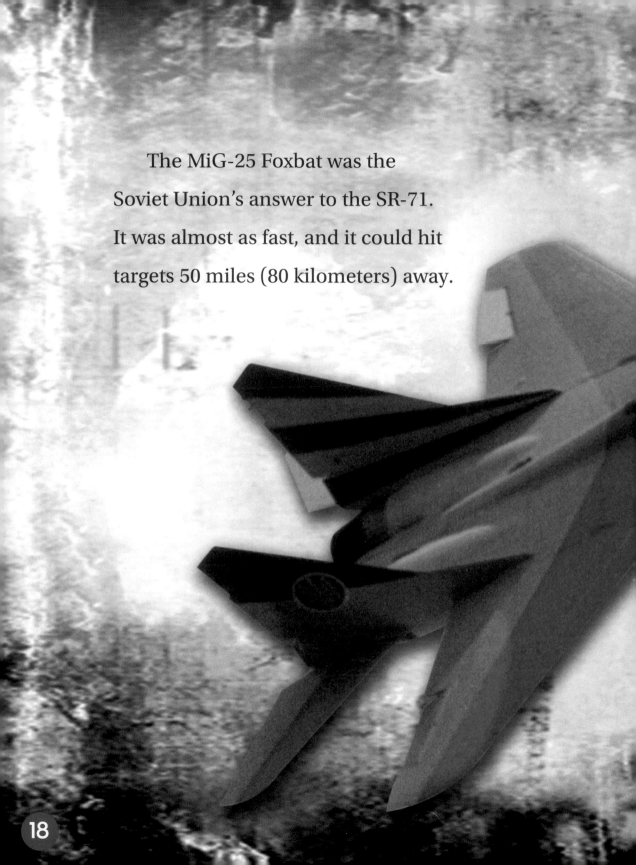

The MiG-25 Foxbat was the
Soviet Union's answer to the SR-71.
It was almost as fast, and it could hit
targets 50 miles (80 kilometers) away.

MiG-29UB Fulcrum

WEAPON FACT

The MiG-29 was an improved version of the MiG-25. It had more advanced electronics systems.

The United States built **stealth** airplanes in the 1980s. The F-117 Nighthawk and the B-2 Spirit were hard for enemy **radar** to see.

stealth — describes aircraft with bodies that make it hard for radar to detect them

radar — a system that detects objects using sound waves

F-117 Nighthawk

B-2 Spirit

WINGED WEAPONS

MiG-25 Foxbat

B-1 bomber

B-2 Spirit bomber

F-117A Nighthawk stealth fighter

SR-71 spy plane

MiG-29UB Fulcrum

U-2 spy plane

MiG-17 fighter

B-52G Stratofortress bomber

WEAPON FACT

The Soviet Union began launching satellites into space in 1957.

DEFENSE PLANS

Spy **satellites** for both countries circled the earth. They snapped detailed photographs of enemy actions.

satellite — a spacecraft that circles the earth

Both countries had strong defense systems. Missiles and **Kinetic Kill Vehicles (KKVs)** could destroy enemy weapons and aircraft.

Kinetic Kill Vehicle (KKV) – a warhead shot at ultra-high speeds

WEAPON FACT

U.S. Patriot missiles could shoot down aircraft and missiles that flew faster than the speed of sound.

U.S. Patriot missile

launchpad

Bunkers were the last line of defense. These huge underground shelters were built to protect people from nuclear attacks. Luckily, they were never needed. The cold war ended in 1989.

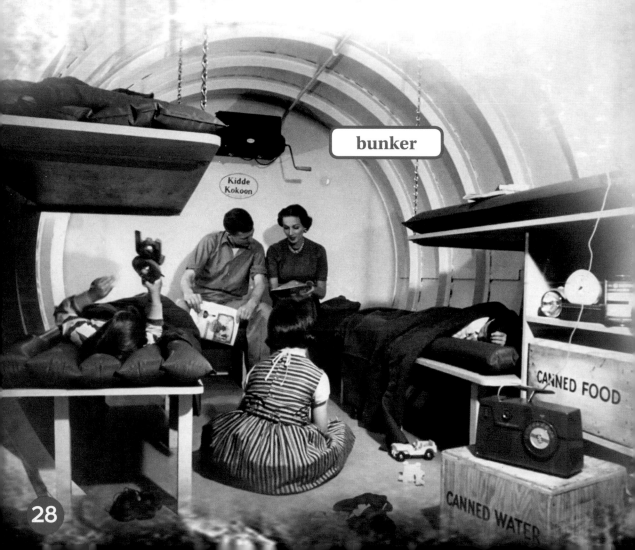

bunker

DRASTIC DEFENSES

bunker

satellite

anti-satellite missile

Patriot missile

GLOSSARY

ballistic missile (buh-LISS-tik MISS-uhl) — a missile that is powered as it climbs, but falls freely

bunker (BUHNG-kuhr) — an underground shelter from bomb attacks and gunfire

Kinetic Kill Vehicle (ki-NET-ik KIL VEE-uh-kuhl) — a weapon shot at high speeds that can stop enemy missiles

nuclear bomb (NOO-klee-ur BOM) — a powerful explosive that destroys large areas; nuclear bombs leave behind harmful elements called radiation.

radar (RAY-dar) — equipment that uses radio waves to find and guide objects

satellite (SAT-uh-lite) — a spacecraft that circles the earth; satellites gather and send information.

stealth (STELTH) — the ability to move without being detected

warhead (WOR-hed) — the explosive part of a missile or rocket

READ MORE

Bodden, Valerie. *The Cold War.* Days of Change. Mankato, Minn.: Creative Education, 2008.

Grant, R. G. *The Cold War.* Timelines. Mankato, Minn.: Arcturus, 2008.

Stanley, George E. *America and the Cold War (1949–1969).* Primary Source History of the United States. Milwaukee: World Almanac, 2005.

INTERNET SITES

FactHound offers a safe, fun way to find educator-approved Internet sites related to this book.

Here's what you do:

1. Visit *www.facthound.com*

2. Choose your grade level.

3. Begin your search.

This book's ID number is 9781429623322.

FactHound will fetch the best sites for you!

INDEX